Steven Appleby's
ABC of CHILDHOOD

Bloomsbury

Steven Appleby's

ABC of

CHILDHOOD

MOST OF THE CARTOONS IN THIS BOOK
FIRST APPEARED IN **JUNIOR** MAGAZINE

First published in Great Britain in 2005
Copyright © 2005 Steven Appleby
The moral right of the author has been asserted
Bloomsbury Publishing PLC, 38 Soho Sq, London W1D 3HB
A CIP catalogue record for this book is available
from the British Library.
ISBN 0 7475 7604 1

10 9 8 7 6 5 4 3 2 1

Printed and bound by C+C Offset Printing Co., Ltd., Hong Kong

All papers used by Bloomsbury Publishing are natural,
recyclable products made from wood grown in well-managed
forests. The manufacturing processes conform to the
environmental regulations of the country of origin.
http://www.bloomsbury.com/stevenappleby

For Jasper, Clem & Stanley

APPLE-OF-ONE'S-EYE

ADORATION

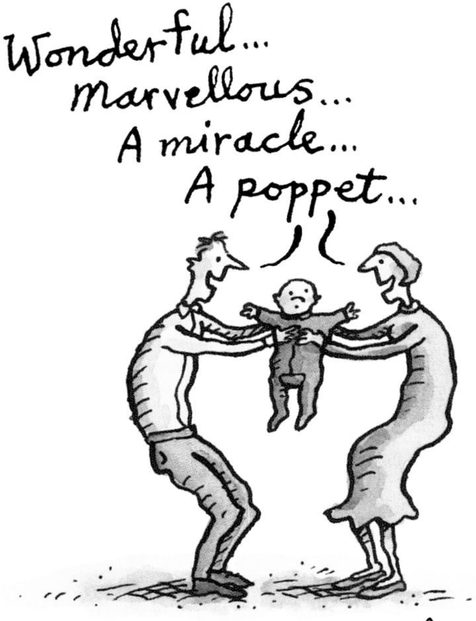

COMING NEXT: **B** is for DOWN-TO-EARTH-WITH-A **BUMP**.

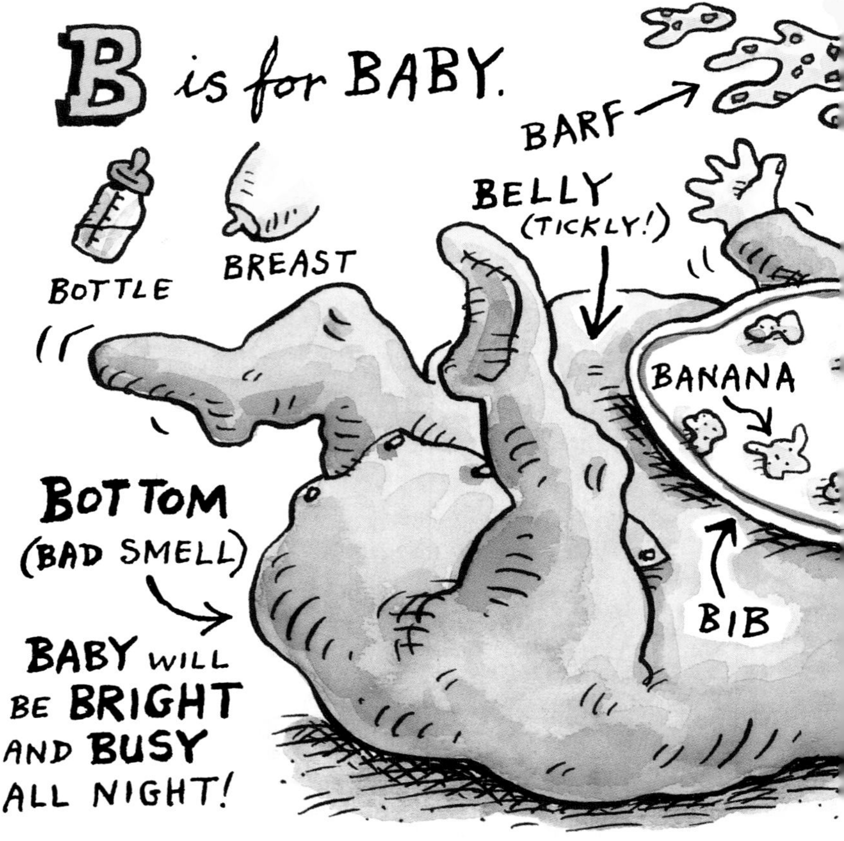
B is for BABY.
BARF
BOTTLE
BREAST
BELLY
(TICKLY!)
BANANA
BOTTOM
(BAD SMELL)
BIB
BABY WILL
BE BRIGHT
AND BUSY
ALL NIGHT!

BABYSITTER
Our first night out since Montgomery was born! I can't wait!
DING DONG!
Here's the babysitter.
SOON...
He likes to be rocked...
WAAAAA!
ROCKING
He likes you to sing!
Baa baa black sheep...
WAAA!!
WAAA!

C is for CLAIRVOYANCE.

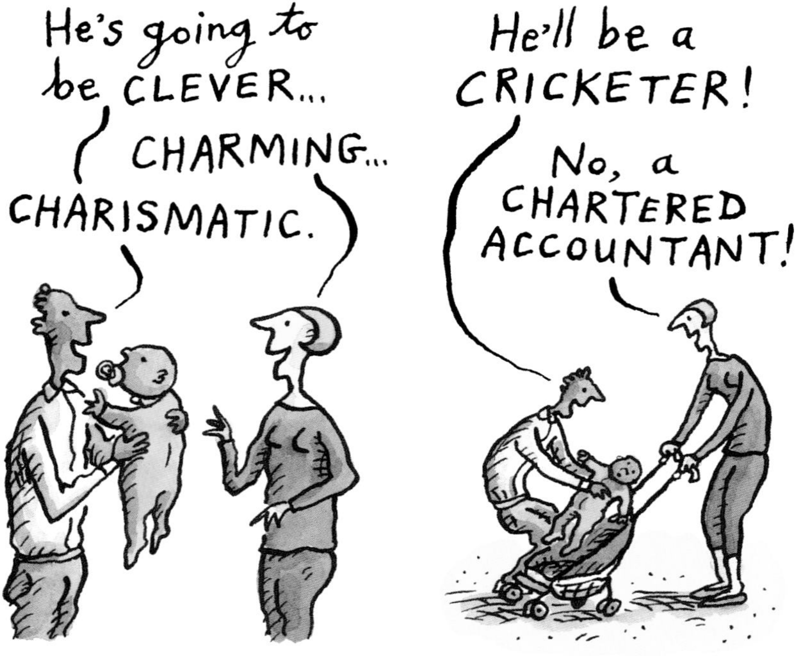

A COSMONAUT!
A CHIP-SHOP OWNER!
A CHILD PSYCHOLOGIST!
A CHIPMUNK HANDLER!
Anything, just so long as he isn't a CARTOONIST!
Gosh, yes! There's no CASH in that!

D is for DUMMY.

I'm off out.

Wait! How do I keep Molly DOCILE, DORMANT and DIVINE?

Give her a DUMMY.

E is for EDUCATION.

It's never *too* early to start!

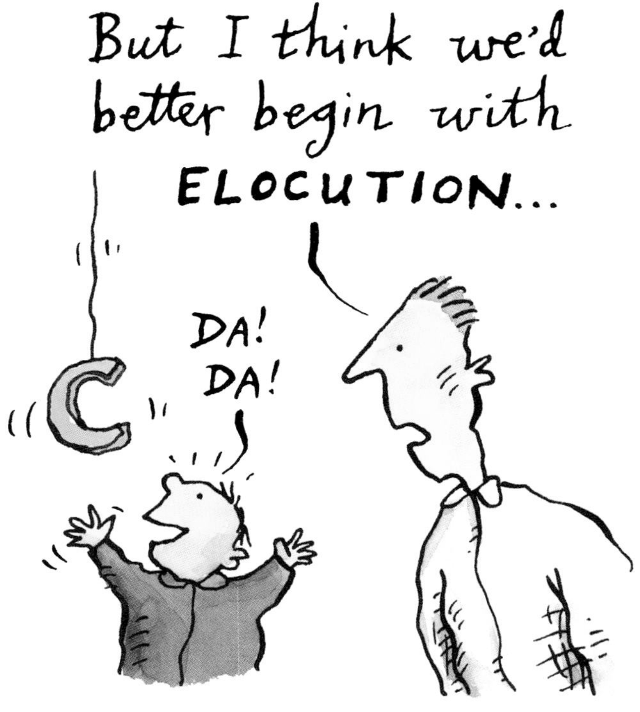
But I think we'd better begin with ELOCUTION...
DA! DA!

F is for FIRST WORDS.

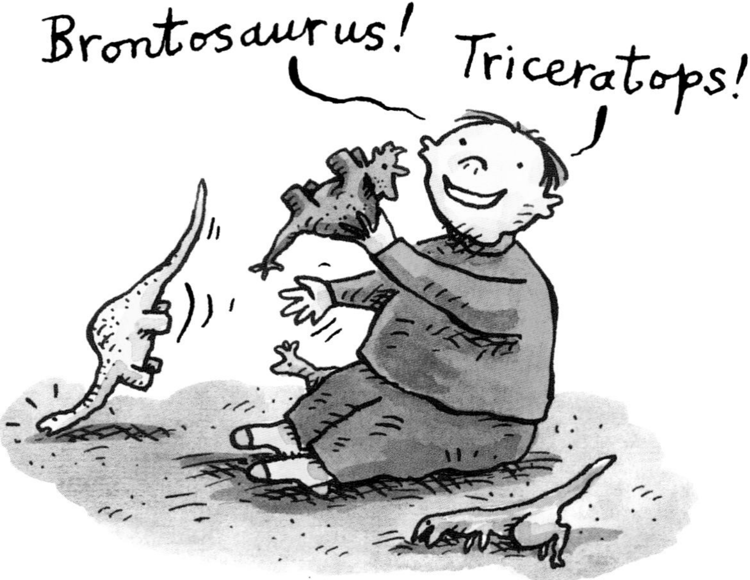

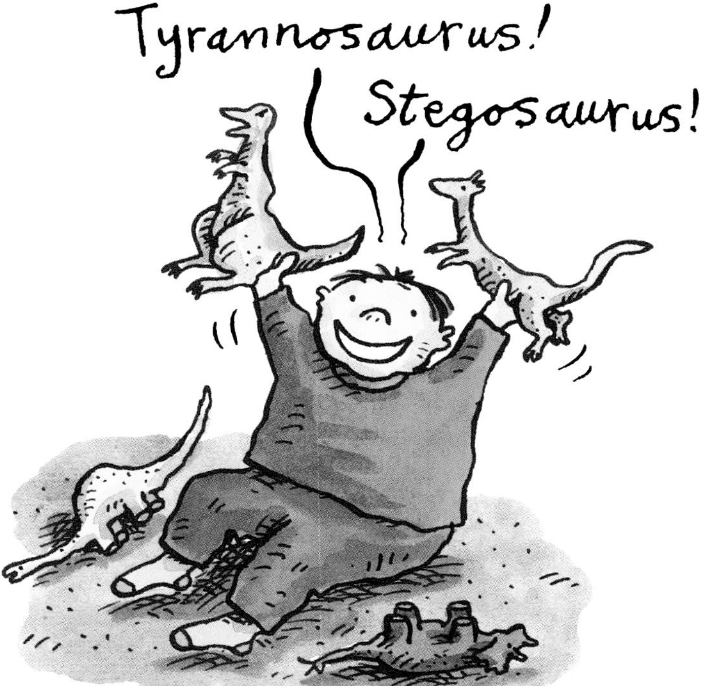
Tyrannosaurus!
Stegosaurus!

FUSSPOT

FIONA FRANKENSTEIN IS
A FUSSY CHILD.

Want different food!
Want a different plate!
Want a different
drink!

iv — A BABY INTO WHICH YOU
CAN INSERT DVDs AND VIDEOS

v — A BABY PRE-PROGRAMMED
WITH THE ABILITY TO SAY:

Teletubbies!
Noddy!
Pingu!
AND TWENTY
OTHER KIDS'
FAVOURITES

MORE GENETIC MODIFICATION...

I agree with you, but I think children should be NOT SEEN, too.
So I specified that Megan should be invisible.
WHISPER
Hello!

H is for HOTHOUSING.

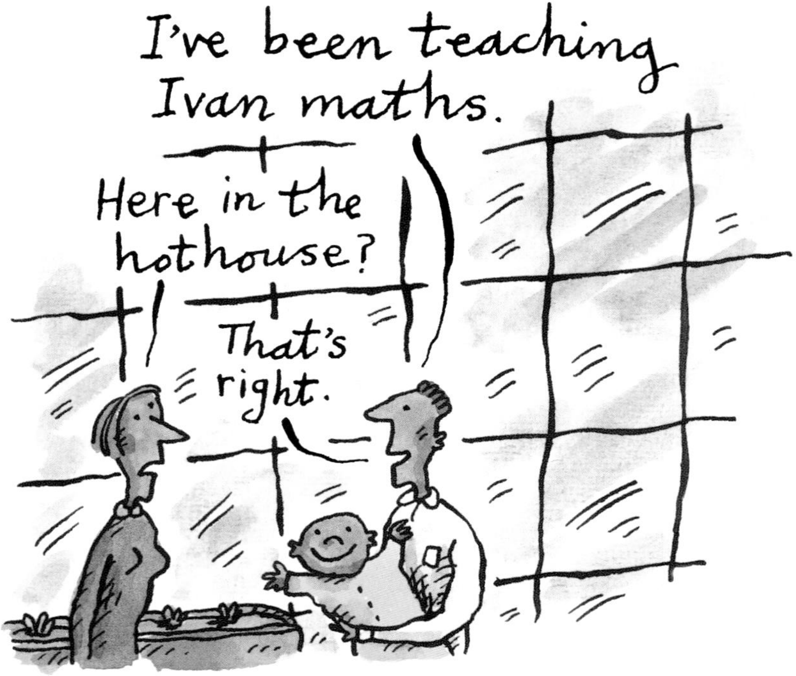

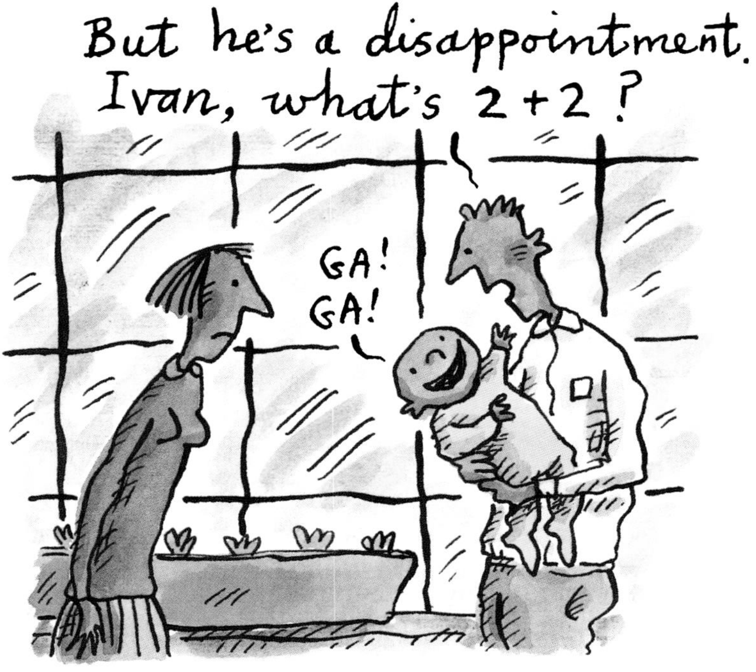
But he's a disappointment.
Ivan, what's 2 + 2 ?
GA!
GA!

On the other hand I'm very proud of the tomatoes.
The answer's FOUR!
Ask us another.

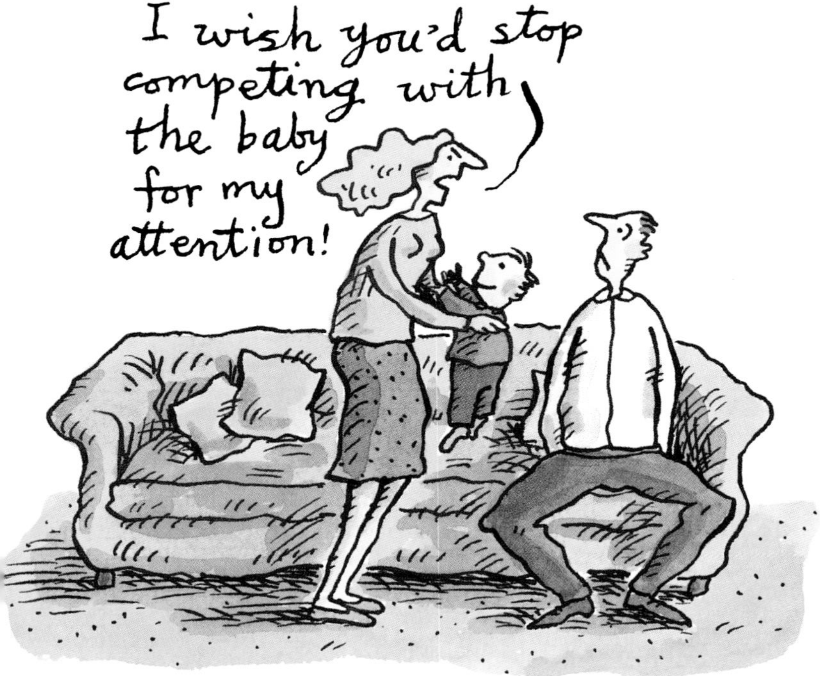
I wish you'd stop competing with the baby for my attention!

ILLNESSES ~ OF CHILDREN
NUMBER 1: PRETENDING

SYMPTOMS (BEFORE 9.00 AM ON A SCHOOLDAY):

GROAN...
MOAN...
WHINGE...

I've got a headache...

My tummy hurts...

I feel sick...

Ooh... My leg is sore.

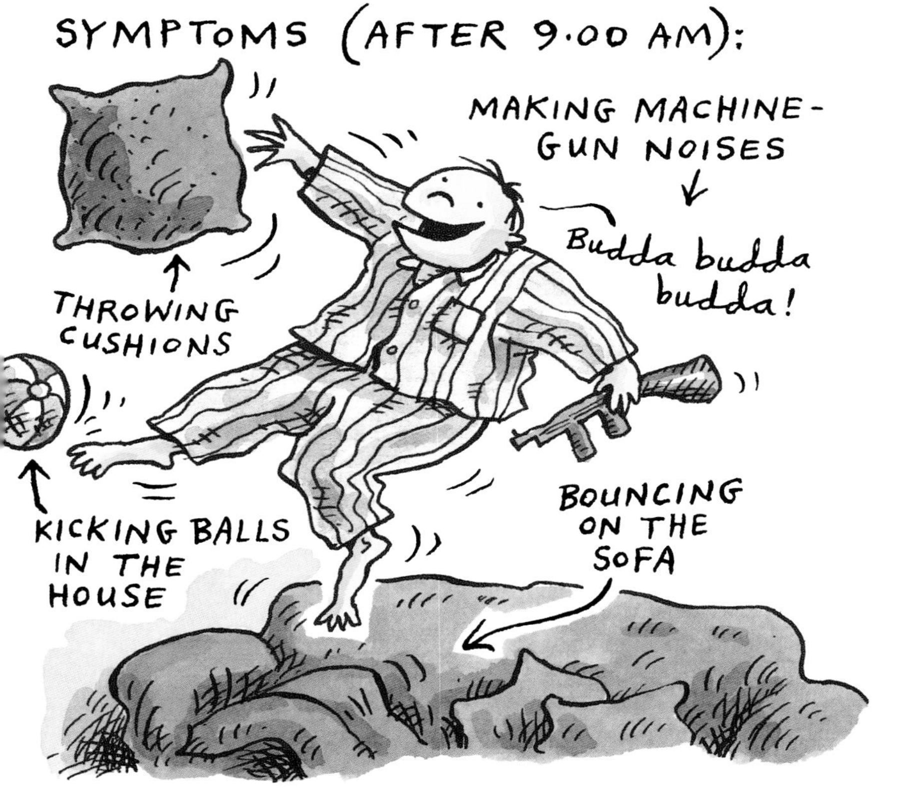
SYMPTOMS (AFTER 9.00 AM):
MAKING MACHINE-GUN NOISES
Budda budda budda!
THROWING CUSHIONS
KICKING BALLS IN THE HOUSE
BOUNCING ON THE SOFA

ILLNESSES ~ OF PARENTS
NUMBER 1: BAD BACK

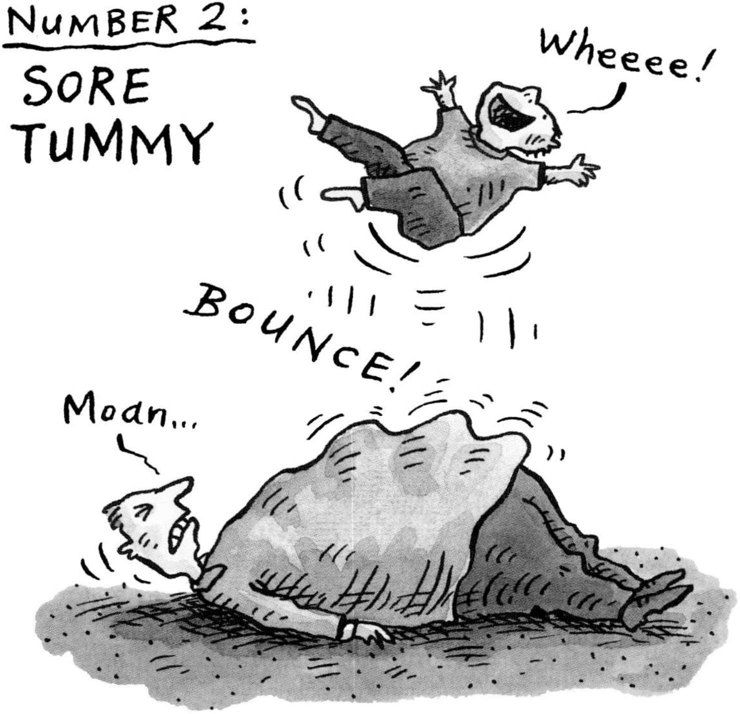
NUMBER 2:
SORE TUMMY
Wheeeee!
BOUNCE!
Moan...

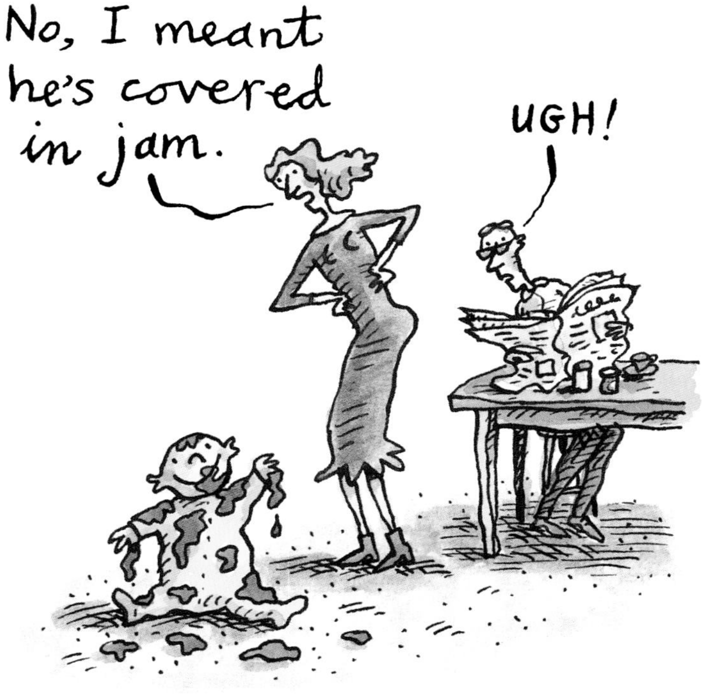
No, I meant he's covered in jam.
UGH!

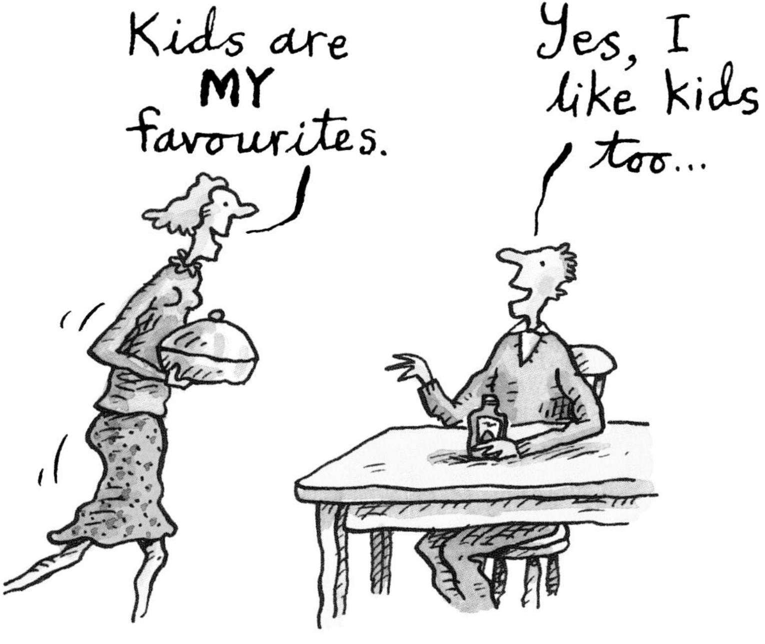
Kids are **MY** favourites.
Yes, I like kids too...

L is for LIMERICK... and LIES!

THERE WAS A SMALL
BOY WHO TOLD LIES.

Who's eaten ALL
the chocolate
spread with a
spoon?!

WHICH, WHEN
FACED WITH,
HE ALWAYS
DENIED.

Not me!

HE WOULD RAGE
TEARFULLY...

You're just
picking on
me!

BUT THE
EVIDENCE
PROVED
OTHERWISE.

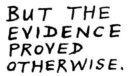

NOT FAIR!

STAMP!
STAMP!

M is for MONSTERS!

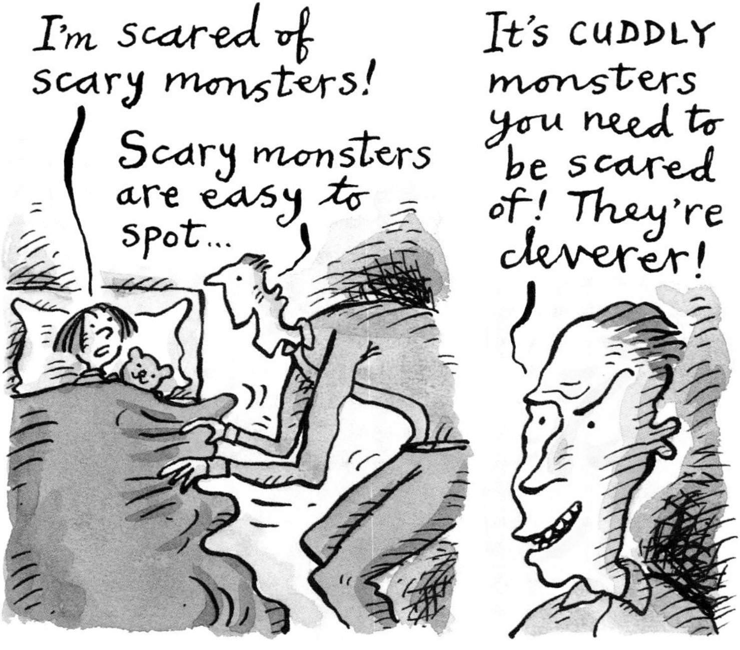

They gain your confidence, make you love them, then - when you least expect it - SNAP!!
They tear your head off!
So Teddy might be...
Yup. Night night.

N is for NAMES.

My three girls are called Faith, Hope and Charity.

You see, I believe that a name can help form a child's character, thus guiding them through life.
Oh, I totally agree!

NEGOTIATION

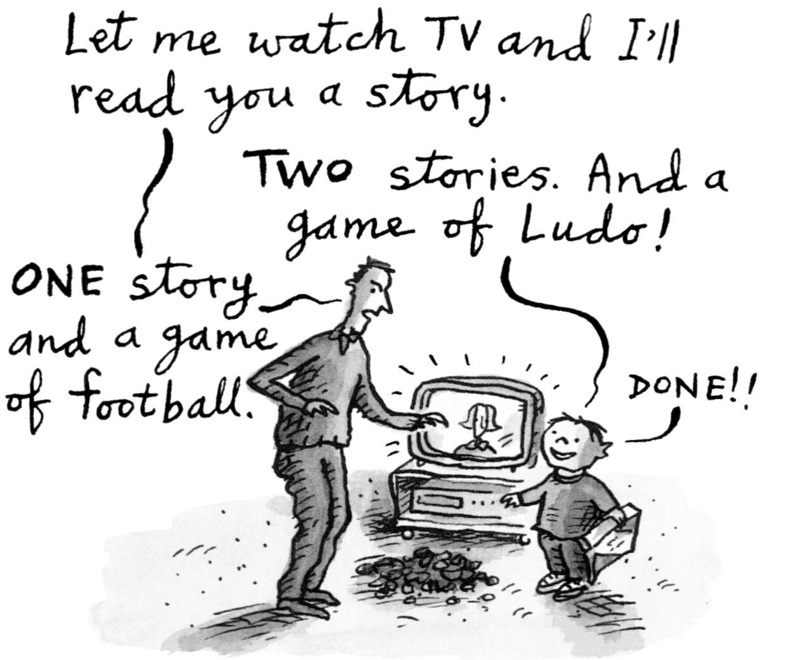

O is for ODD.

Ogdred is an odd little boy.
You're right.
There are TWO Bartlet twins but only ONE Ogdred and one is an ODD number.
I meant odd in other ways, too.

True. He's got THREE arms, FIVE legs and SEVEN heads. More odd numbers.
Good day, Earthlings. How are you?
He's very polite, though.
Well brought up.

P is for PLAY.

POTTY TRAINING

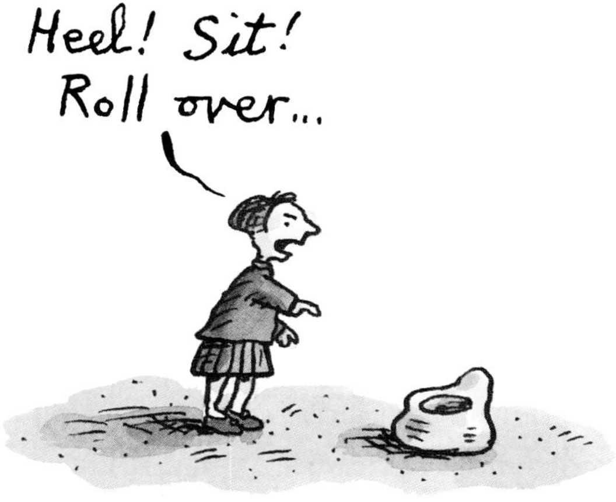
Heel! Sit!
Roll over...

Q *is for* QUEENSBERRY RULES.

ONE MORNING AT PLAYGROUP...

R is for RICH GIRL'S RHINOCEROS.

And they're an endangered species. She'd learn about conservation, too.
True.
SOON...
Aw, Fido is sitting on Sophia's lap!
How sweet!
Fetch, Boy!

S is for SIX WAYS TO SAY

1- VERY QUIETLY

(sorry...)

I didn't hear that!

2 - TACTICALLY

Sorry.

You're only saying that so I let you off lightly!

"I'M SORRY!"

3-AGGRESSIVELY!

4 — ROUTINELY

5 – MEANING THE COMPLETE OPPOSITE-LY
Sor-ry!
6 – GENUINELY
I'm sorry.
She's FINALLY said it as if she means it!
My God! What must she have done?!

SUGAR AND SPICE
AND ALL THINGS NICE...

Maisie LOVES sugar.

Sugar is bad for her, though.

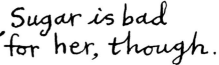

T is for THERAPY.

PARENTS, BUY THESE T-SHIRTS FOR YOUR KIDS! YOU'LL SOON FEEL WANTED AND WORTHWHILE.

TIMESHARE

CHILDREN:

WORK:

HOUSEWORK:

PERSONAL SPACE:

SLAP SLAP

HUSBAND:
What about time for me?
FEELING NEGLECTED
Behave! You're a grown man. You can look after yourself.

TRIPLETS

 **V** is for VIDEOS.

Turn that thing **OFF**! Stop watching videos and play a good, healthy game in the REAL WORLD! Use your **OWN** imagination for a change!

LATER...

What are you doing now?

I've used my imagination to make a PRETEND TV and I'm watching Bugs Bunny on it.

W is for WAIT!

Mum always says "wait". Watch this.

I want some chocolate!

Wait until after supper.

I want to try your wine!

Wait until you grow up.

I want a water buffalo!

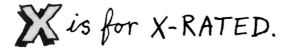 **is for X-RATED.**

Y is for YIN and YANG.

When YIN and YANG are in perfect balance everything seems rosy.

At other times it must be very hard work having twins.

Z is for ZOMBIE.

Being a parent has turned me into a complete ZOMBIE, which means I have ZERO ideas for this page.

THE AUTHOR

YOUR baby's pages...

STICK BABY
PICTURE HERE

BABY'S NAME _____

DATE OF BIRTH _____

PLACE OF BIRTH _____

TIME OF BIRTH _____

SEX: M ☐ F ☐ ? ☐ STAR SIGN _____

WEIGHT _____ LENGTH _____

WHO WAS AT BIRTH _____

_____

_____

_____

GORY DETAILS _____

_____

HAIR ☐ NO HAIR ☐ HAIR COLOUR _____
EYEBROWS ☐ NO EYEBROWS ☐

TEMPERAMENT: GRUMPY ☐ PLACID ☐
HAPPY ☐ CROSS ☐ BEWILDERED ☐

NOISE LEVEL: 0 |⌶⌶⌶⌶⌶⌶⌶⌶⌶⌶⌶| 10
                          5

BODYSHAPE: SKINNY ☐ PLUMP ☐ PORKY ☐

FIRST SMILE _____

FIRST SOLID FOOD _____

FIRST SWEETS _____

FIRST CHIPS _____

FIRST CHOC SPREAD _____

FIRST TANTRUM _____

FIRST POO IN POTTY_____

FIRST WORDS _____

_____

_____

_____

_____

_____

_____

FIRST TOOTH _____

FIRST CRAWLED _____

FIRST WALKED _____

FIRST SLEPT THROUGH NIGHT_____

FAVOURITE FOOD _____

_____

_____

FAVOURITE DVDs _____

_____

_____

FAVOURITE BOOKS _____

_____

_____

_____

THE AUTHOR, AGE 2